To:

From:

Date:

The Beautiful Word for Christmas

Copyright © 2017 by Zondervan

Requests for information should be addressed to:

Zondervan, 3900 Sparks Dr., SE, Grand Rapids, MI 49546

ISBN 978-0-3100-8756-4

The Scripture on pages 4–49 is from Luke 1:26-38 and 2:1-21.

Unless otherwise indicated, Scripture quotations are taken from the Holy Bible, New International Version®, NIV® Copyright ©1973, 1978, 1984, 2011 by Biblica, Inc.® Used by permission. All rights reserved worldwide.

Scriptures marked NASB are taken from the New American Standard Bible®, Copyright © 1960, 1962, 1963, 1968, 1971, 1972, 1973, 1975, 1977, 1995 by The Lockman Foundation. Used by permission. (www.Lockman.org)

Scriptures marked NKJV are taken from the New King James Version®. Copyright © 1982 by Thomas Nelson. Used by permission. All rights reserved.

Scriptures marked NLT are taken from the *Holy Bible*, New Living Translation, copyright © 1996, 2004, 2015 by Tyndale House Foundation. Used by permission of Tyndale House Publishers Inc., Carol Stream, Illinois 60188. All rights reserved.

Any Internet addresses (websites, blogs, etc.) and telephone numbers in this book are offered as a resource. They are not intended in any way to be or imply an endorsement by Zondervan, nor does Zondervan vouch for the content of these sites and numbers for the life of this book.

Cover design: Kristi Smith of Juicebox Designs

Interior hand-lettering and illustration: Kristi Smith of Juicebox Design (pages 4-9, 16-21, 28-33, 40-47) and Kerri Charlton (pages 10-15, 22-27, 34-39, 48, 49)

Interior design: Koechel Peterson & Associates, Mpls. MN

Printed in China

17 18 19 20 21 22 23 /LEO/ 22 21 20 19 18 17 16 15 14 13 12 11 10 9 8 7 6 5 4 3 2 1

The Beautiful WORD™ for Christmas

to BRING the JOY of ADVENT to YOUR HEART

ZONDERVAN®
.com

In the SIXTH month of Elizabeth's PREGNANCY, God SENT THE angel Gabriel to Nazareth, a TOWN in Galilee,

to a virgin PLEDGED to be MARRIED to a man NAMED JOSEPH, a DESCENDANT of David.

The virgin's name was

Mary.

The ANGEL went to HER and said,

"GREETINGS, *you who are highly* FAVORED! *The* LORD *is* WITH YOU."

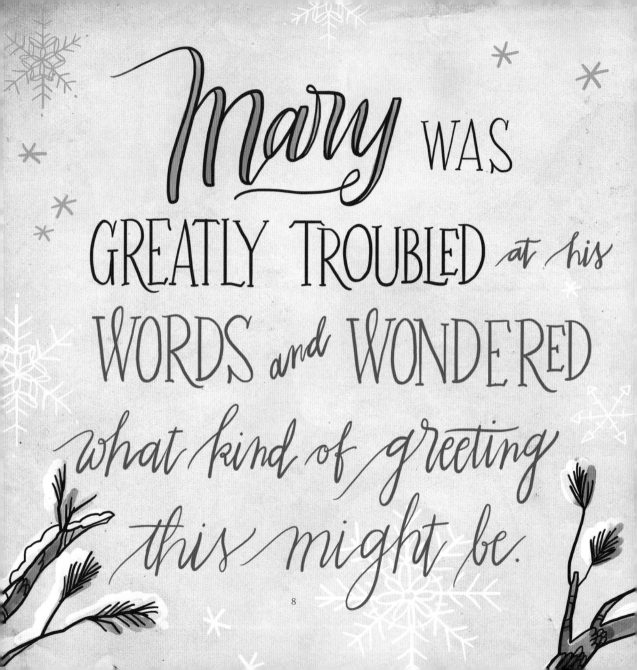

Mary WAS GREATLY TROUBLED at his WORDS and WONDERED what kind of greeting this might be.

8

BUT the ANGEL SAID to HER, "Do not be afraid, Mary; YOU HAVE FOUND FAVOR WITH GOD.

YOU WILL CONCEIVE
AND GIVE BIRTH
TO A SON,
AND YOU ARE
TO CALL HIM

Jesus.

HE WILL BE *great* AND WILL BE CALLED THE *Son* OF THE *Most High.*

11

The
Lord God will give him

DAV

the throne of his father

VID,

and he will reign over Jacob's descendants forever; his kingdom will never end."

"How will this be," Mary asked the angel,

"SINCE I AM A VIRGIN?"

The angel answered, "The **HOLY SPIRIT** WILL COME ON YOU, and the **POWER** of the **MOST HIGH** WILL OVERSHADOW YOU.

16

So the *holy one* to be BORN WILL BE CALLED the SON of GOD.

EVEN Elizabeth your relative is going to have a CHILD in her old age, and she who was said to be unable to conceive is in her sixth month.

For no word from God will ever fail."

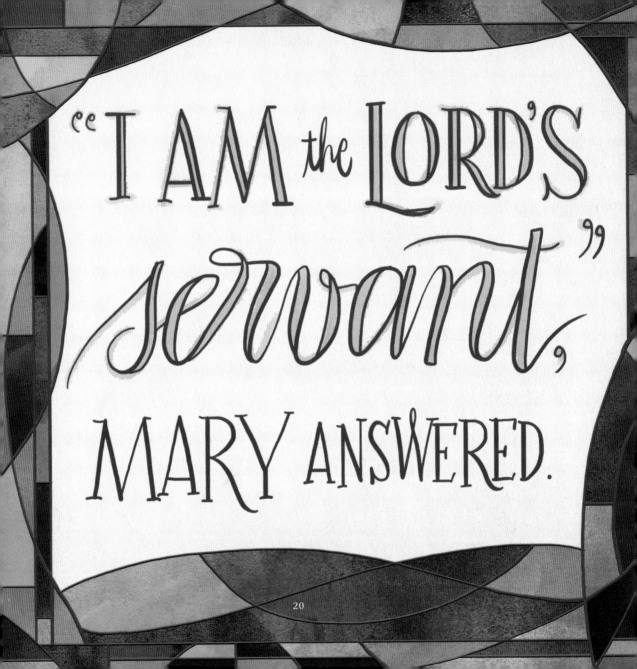

"I AM the LORD'S servant," MARY ANSWERED.

20

"May your word to me BE FULFILLED." THEN the ANGEL left her.

In those days Caesar Augustus issued a decree that a census should be taken of the entire Roman world . . . .

AND
EVERYONE
WENT TO
THEIR OWN
TOWN TO
REGISTER.

So Joseph also went up from the town of Nazareth in Galilee to Judea, to Bethlehem the town of David, because he belonged to the house and line of David.

He went there to register
with Mary, who was pledged
to be married to him
and was expecting a child.

26

27

while they were there,
the TIME CAME
for the
BABY to be BORN,

28

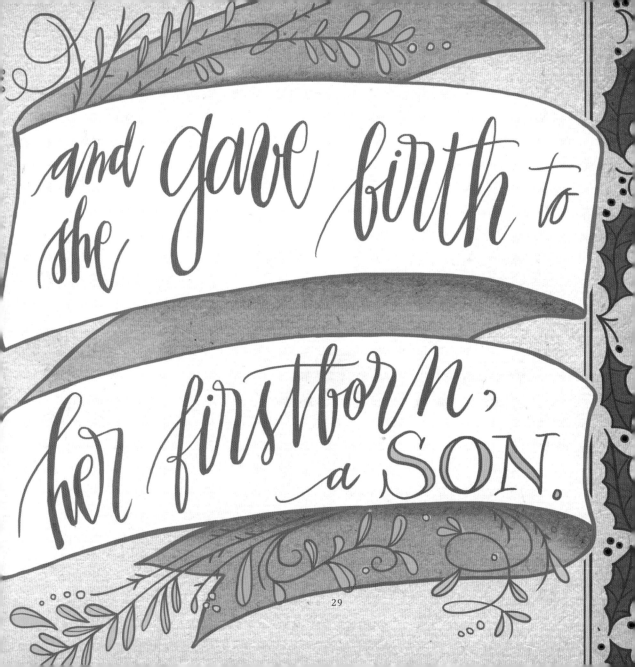

and she gave birth to her firstborn, a SON.

SHE WRAPPED HIM IN CLOTHS AND PLACED HIM IN A MANGER,

BECAUSE THERE WAS NO GUEST ROOM AVAILABLE FOR THEM.

and there were SHEPHERDS living out in the FIELDS NEARBY,

keeping watch
over their
FLOCKS at NIGHT.

An angel of the Lord
appeared to them, and the

glory

of the Lord

shone around them,
and they were terrified.

BUT, THE ANGEL
SAID TO THEM,

"DO NOT BE AFRAID.

I BRING YOU

GOOD NEWS

THAT WILL CAUSE

GREAT JOY FOR

ALL THE PEOPLE."

Today in the town of David a Savior has been born to you; he is the Messiah, the Lord.

"This will be a sign to you: You will find a baby wrapped in cloths and lying in a manger."

SUDDENLY a GREAT COMPANY of the HEAVENLY HOST appeared with the ANGEL, PRAISING GOD and SAYING,

"Glory to God in the highest heaven, and on earth PEACE to those on whom his favor rests."

WHEN the ANGELS had left them and GONE into HEAVEN, the shepherds said to one another,

"Let's go to Bethlehem

and **see** this thing that has happened,

WHICH THE **LORD** [43] has **TOLD US ABOUT.** "

SO THEY HURRIED OFF and FOUND
MARY and JOSEPH, and the BABY,
WHO WAS LYING in the MANGER.

When they had seen him,
THEY SPREAD the WORD
concerning what had been told

them about THIS CHILD, AND ALL WHO HEARD IT were *amazed* AT WHAT *the* SHEPHERDS SAID *to* THEM.

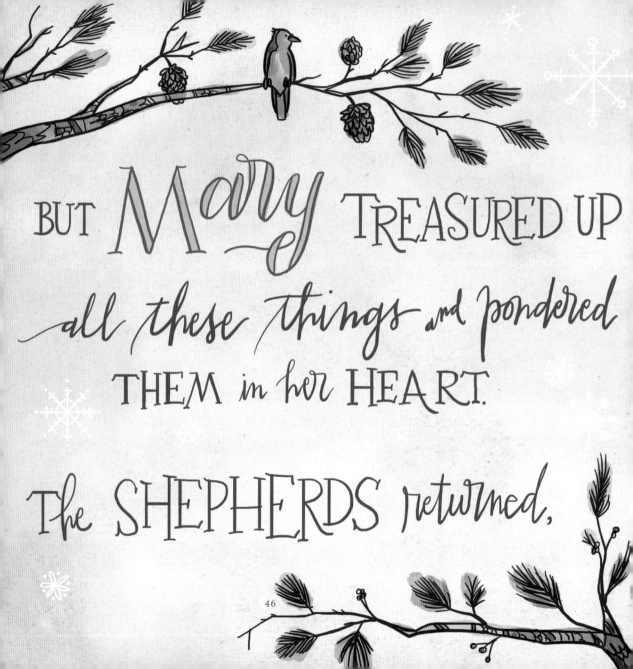

BUT *Mary* TREASURED UP
all these things and pondered
THEM in her HEART.

The SHEPHERDS returned,

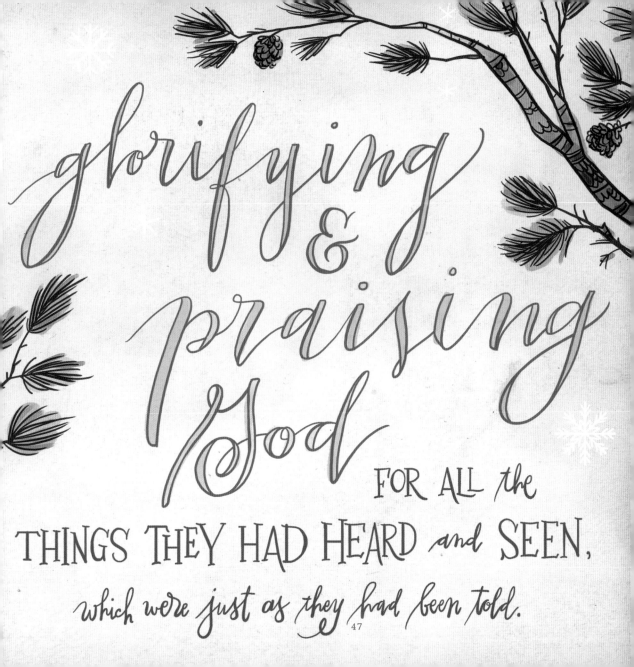

glorifying & praising God FOR ALL the THINGS THEY HAD HEARD and SEEN, which were just as they had been told.

On the eighth day,
when it was time to
circumcise the child,

he was named

Jesus

the name the angel had given him before he was conceived.

This collection of devotions was written to help you navigate the wonder-filled—but often stress-filled—season of Advent. In these devotions, one for each day of December, you will meet women much like yourself, each of whom finds joy and peace or receives answers from God just in time for the holidays. Find encouragement in these devotions, and above all else—in the midst of all the chaos and cacophony that is Christmas—see and enjoy the Babe who is a King.

The Beauty of *Receiving*

Every good and perfect gift is from above,

coming down from the Father of the heavenly lights,

who does not change like shifting shadows.

JAMES 1:17

L ast Christmas, Sarah had opened the semi-heavy box while her family looked on and smiled. Warm boots! For some reason she had always battled terribly cold feet, even in summer. The condition had been uncomfortable and frustrating, and because of it she had kept the genius who'd invented fuzzy socks in business, for years. But her family had come to the rescue with warm, wool-lined boots.

As she lifted the boots from the box, outwardly Sarah rejoiced. But inside, a little voice taunted her. *You're not worth those expensive boots. They're too pricey. Think of what that money could have provided for your family.*

This guilt and mental torment went on for several hours, until finally Sarah could take it no more. "I'm taking the boots back," she told her husband and children.

"No!" cried one of Sarah's kids. "We bought those for *you*." Once-smiling faces now looked at her forlornly. Sarah's husband shook his head grimly.

"But the money could be used for things we need," Sarah persisted.

Sarah's family was sad. They had recognized her need, her inability to keep icy feet toasty, so they'd given her a gift—a gift they all had sacrificed for. Would she really not keep it?

Eventually Sarah had seen the light. She'd kept the boots, and what a difference it had made. But she had nearly deprived her family of the joy of giving, all because she felt too small to receive something big.

Deep down, it's that feeling of unworthiness that gets many of us into trouble. We forget that Jesus deemed each of us worthy of His sacrifice. Because God created us and formed us in our mothers' wombs, we have intrinsic value. And God loves to give good gifts to His children.

Sarah is indebted to her sweet, caring family. Each day she's newly grateful for their steadfast patience and love on that Christmas morning. They had pressed her to keep the boots, hugging her into the decision and proving she was worthy in their eyes. They had also shown her the extravagance of giving, of loving, and of how beautiful a family can be.

Today Sarah sits with warm feet. In inclement winter weather, she'll never, for as long as the boots last, fear cold toes. Her family's sacrificial gift wraps her feet in warmth, but more than that, the boots remind her—and us all—of the wildly extravagant love of God.

Lord, help me be a good receiver, a grateful opener of gifts. Thank You for making me worthy of Your extravagant gifts. Amen.

Activity

Think of someone who is struggling financially this winter and try to discern what would be an extravagant gift for him or her. If you can't afford the entire gift, consider forming an "extravagant gift coalition" with some friends and blessing that person or family with a big, needed gift. Or perhaps a gift of your time would be just the thing. Sometimes free babysitting for an evening is exactly what someone needs.

> Deep down, it's that feeling of unworthiness that gets many of us into trouble. We forget that Jesus deemed each of us worthy of His sacrifice.

DAY 2

The Prairie
Christmas

And God is able to bless you abundantly,

so that in all things at all times, having all that you need,

you will abound in every good work.

2 Corinthians 9:8

Sasha's family faced a tight Christmas season. Their small family of three—Sasha; her husband, Jack; and their five-year-old daughter, Emily—had recently purchased a house on the promise of what they thought was a solid raise. Only, the raise didn't materialize, and now, every month, they struggled to make their mortgage payment. As Sasha thought about Christmas, her heart sank. How would she be able to make it special?

Thankfully, she'd been reading the *Little House on the Prairie* books with Emily, and they'd just finished the story about the Christmas when little Laura had received only a rag doll, a cup, and some candy as a gift. That gave Sasha a brilliant idea. She would re-create Laura's Christmas!

Just weeks before Christmas, she found a gently used, handmade rag doll at a garage sale. She also found a metal cup at a discount store, and over the next few weeks she saved pocket change to buy the candy for Emily's stocking.

Before she knew it, Christmas had arrived. But instead of feeling dread that Christmas morning, Sasha radiated joy. She didn't focus on what she didn't have, but what she did have: a home, a family, the Lord God Himself, and a God-given gift of creativity. And in the creative activity of giving of herself in this leaner financial season, she found the kind of joy she'd missed in Christmases past, when money hadn't been tight. She realized this Christmas of creativity was itself a gift from God, reminding her that He had already given her so much, and all those blessings could be channeled into her family, particularly her daughter.

On Christmas, they revisited Laura's story, and then Emily opened her presents—*they were just like Laura's!* Emily's eyes lit up as she held the doll to her chest. She carried it with her everywhere she went that day. And she would continue to carry that doll for years. It would be her favorite gift and a cherished memory.

Sasha learned that generous giving doesn't always mean a gift given from an abundance of finances, but that it can mean a gift given from the overflow and creativity of the heart—gifts from a very generous heavenly Father.

God has been so generous with you too. And while you may not have the means to give lavish gifts this Christmas, you always have the ability to give of yourself—with joyful abandon. Even when money is tight and you're struggling to make ends meet, consider finding little bits of excess or some of your time to bless someone else. Giving from your abundance, however small you perceive it, takes away a hoarding mentality. It frees you to live joyfully in the present, even in the midst of trying financial times, particularly at Christmas. In this way, you participate in the great generosity of God, who blesses you abundantly for every good deed.

Lord, help me to be a good manager of the money You've given me, whether great or small. This Christmas, help me to see that it's not how much I spend on gifts, but how much love is behind them—and more importantly, how much time I spend with You. Give me the ability to stretch my dollars, and to ask for Your help as I financially navigate this season. Amen.

Activity

Find a gift from your favorite ministry's Christmas catalog to bless a child around the world. If you have children, involve them in deciding what you'd like to give.

> God has been so generous with you. And while you may not have the means to give lavish gifts this Christmas, you always have the ability to give of yourself—with joyful abandon.

A Different Kind of Advent Calendar

In their hearts humans plan their course,

*but the L*ORD *establishes their steps.*

PROVERBS 16:9

Years ago, Glynnis had hand-made a cloth advent calendar to use during the month of December. For each day, from December 1 to December 24, she had created a pocket where she could insert a small slip of paper on which she had written a family-friendly activity for that day. Each year her children took turns thinking up activities and placing them inside the pockets. Some of these were static dates, such as concerts, Christmas parties and ornament exchanges, time with extended family, and so on. For other, empty dates, she added activities, such as a craft night, where the whole family made homemade gifts for the homeless. Then each day, she pulled out the slip of paper, and her family did the recommended activity for that day. Not only did this keep her calendar organized, but it also provided anticipation of what was coming next—a way to look forward to the whole month of December, not just the few days before Christmas.

Every year, her children looked forward to what they would pull out of the little pockets. They read the Christmas story and the passages from Isaiah that foretold the Messiah's birth. They sang Christmas carols, but not up and down their street; instead, they chose a few people who loved to receive phone calls and belted out holiday classics over the phone. They fashioned snowflakes out of recycled Christmas wrapping paper. One night, they drove around the neighborhood, drinking hot chocolate and listening to Christmas music as they tried to choose the best light display. They made Christmas cookies and delivered them to friends. They decorated their fireplace mantel with branches they'd gathered while on a nature walk. These activities brought Glynnis's family close together, and most everything cost next to nothing. In the meantime, they celebrated one another's presence, building memories for years to come.

The holidays are meant to be not only celebrated, but cherished. Advent is a savoring season—a time of preparing your heart for Emmanuel, God with us. While it's fun to give gifts, that's not the only reason for this unique season. It's a time to slow down, reflect, and consider what Jesus has done. It's also a time to reconnect with your friends and family, spending quality time with them instead of living tethered to a stressful schedule. You may plan your days the way Glynnis did, with her unique Advent calendar, but remember to give God permission to interrupt you at will so you can cherish and enjoy the season.

Jesus, help me prepare well for Your coming this Christmas. Whatever method You bring my way, I want to honor You, be responsive to You, and learn the art of cherishing You as we near Your birthday. Protect me from letting busyness usurp my joy. Instead, give me the wherewithal to ponder, to gather my family together, and to slow down enough to relish each moment of this special season. Amen.

Activity

Set aside one day during December for rejuvenation before Christmas. Spend quiet time together with your loved ones—no TV, phones, or electronics. Go outside. Hike. Enjoy the day. And think about the incarnation: that Jesus left the glory of heaven and chose to enter into time and space and gritty earth—for *your* sake. Let this day be a day of preparation for you, preparing you to celebrate—from the heart—the wonder of Christ's birth.

> The holidays are meant to be not only celebrated, but cherished. Advent is a savoring season—a time of preparing your heart for Emmanuel, God with us.

DAY 4

The Great
Exchange

In your relationships with one another, have the same

mindset as Christ Jesus: Who, being in very nature God, did

not consider equality with God something to be used to his

own advantage; rather, he made himself nothing by taking

the very nature of a servant, being made in human likeness.

PHILIPPIANS 2:5–7

Jerushah had grown tired of the commercialism so rampant around the holidays. Before Halloween had even ended, stores were already reminding her of tinsel, Santa, and a rush of obligations she felt too tired to meet. She had a full life, with relationships in several spheres—coworkers, church friends, family, and neighbors. This year, she wanted to celebrate them all, but she couldn't wrap her mind around how to do that.

A neighbor, Tammy, reminded her of a simple way to celebrate people and also keep her heart centered on Jesus: an exchange! So Jerushah participated in four different exchanges.

At work, she and her coworkers did an ornament exchange. Everyone brought a single, pretty, gift-wrapped ornament and numbered it. Then each person drew a number and could either open the corresponding gift or choose another.

With her small group from church, Jerushah participated in a time exchange at their leader's home. With Christmas music playing in the background and goodies on the table, the group just hung out while everyone tackled their holiday tasks—writing and addressing Christmas cards, making bows, and wrapping presents.

To keep expenses low, Jerushah did a name exchange with her cousins, aunts, and uncles, limiting the gifts to five dollars or less, allowing for thrifted and creative gifts.

Tammy hosted a meal exchange for Jerushah's neighborhood. To make it easier, Tammy first purchased some throwaway containers at a local dollar store. Then she invited her neighbors who enjoyed cooking to spend two hours together in the kitchen, each creating a main dish that would serve a number of people. The night of the exchange, neighbors each made a dish, distributed it among several containers, then left with the same number of different main dishes. Jerushah went home with six dinners—a true blessing during a busy season.

Perhaps you are participating in several "exchanges" yourself this Christmas season. If so, in light of all these exchanges, it's important that you recognize the most important exchange of all. Jesus, in His deity, exchanged heaven's beauty for earth's soil. Consider the humility it must have taken for Him to do this—not only to exchange ethereal for earthly, but glory for death. Paul reminded us of this in today's reading from Philippians.

Jesus made this exchange for your sake, so you could live and breathe and love well on this earth. As you exchange gifts or food or time this Christmas season, remember that Jesus came to earth to exchange His life for yours.

Jesus, I don't always comprehend the exchange You offered on my behalf, but I do understand the joy I receive when I give to others. That must be how You felt when You came to earth to give us Yourself. Help me remember that beautiful exchange this holiday when I exchange gifts. Amen.

Activity

If you're rushed this season and feel too overwhelmed to plan an exchange, give yourself permission to be casual. Simply invite four friends over to bake alongside you. Each should bring a recipe, some ingredients, and a smile.

Jesus, in His deity, exchanged heaven's beauty for earth's soil. Consider the humility it must have taken for Him to do this—to not only exchange ethereal for earthly, but glory for death.

DAY 5

The Friendship Brunch

A friend is always loyal, and a brother is

born to help in time of need.

PROVERBS 17:17 NLT

Every year, around Christmas, Charity hosts a friendship brunch. She strategically thinks over the year and ruminates on the friends God has brought into her life. She hosts a different mixture of people every year, some cherished, long-standing friendships, along with new people she's met over the year. She typically does this on a Saturday in early December, but she prays through how she will bless those friends all year long.

One year God reminded her of this verse: "Do not let kindness and truth leave you; bind them around your neck, write them on the tablet of your heart" (Proverbs 3:3 NASB). So, Charity found an online charm maker and had charms made bearing the words *kindness* and *truth*. Her friends wore those charms around their necks the following year.

Each year, before her friendship brunch, Charity sets the table and decorates it. She wants this time to be a respite, a bright spot in a busy month. She bakes simple coffee cake and egg dishes and makes sparkling drinks from seltzer and cranberry juice.

The best part of the brunch comes when her guests take a moment to share how the past year went for them. Sometimes Charity asks each friend to tell what was the high point of the year—and the low. Other times, the sharing is more organic. But everyone gets a turn. Sometimes people cry. Oftentimes they'll laugh. But through it all, everyone connects.

Who has God placed in your path this year? How can you take a moment to bless them? Simply texting and telling a friend you're thankful for her in your life will change the tenor of her day. Sending a quick note would really bless her. Saying why you like her on her Facebook page will show her you're thinking about her.

Christmas is a time to celebrate relationships with our families and friends, but it's also a time to herald God's faithfulness to us in relationship. Look back over your year. How has God proven Himself faithful to you? What have been your highs and lows, and how has God intersected them? What relationships has God brought into your life?

As you reflect, remember that your relationship with Jesus is the best relationship you have. He is your perfect best friend. He knows you better than your bestie, and He loves you through any and every trial you'll face in the coming year. What a gift He is to you!

Jesus, help me to celebrate You this upcoming season. I want to be a thankful person, thankful not only for my friends and family, but for You and the gifts You give me. Thank You for sending so many significant relationships my way this year. Give me insight as to how I can bless my friends in a tangible way. Amen.

Activity

Write a letter to a significant friend in your life, detailing what you appreciate about her and why you admire her. Instead of mailing it, ask to go out to coffee; then read the letter to her. This may end up being the most significant gift you give this year.

Remember that your relationship with Jesus is the best relationship you have. He is your perfect best friend. He knows you better than your bestie, and He loves you through any and every trial you'll face in the coming year.

DAY 6

Choose to Invite Jesus

For we are God's masterpiece.

He has created us anew in Christ Jesus,

so we can do the good things he planned for us long ago.

Ephesians 2:10 NLT

God has created us all as creatures able to connect with their Creator. The Greek word for *masterpiece* in this verse is *poiema*, from which we get our word *poem*. We are the poetry of God, the creative expression of Him. He speaks to a dying world through the poetry of you, and He fashions you daily into a masterpiece—a stunning creative work from His hand. The beauty of our Creator is that He loves to create.

Since He is the Master, and we are His masterpieces, why would we ever believe monotony is the way to His heart? In *Windows of the Soul*, author Ken Gire reminds us, "We reach for God in many ways. Through our sculptures and our scriptures. Through our pictures and our prayers. Through our writing and our worship. And through them, He reaches for us."

How can you live in the light of this creativity, especially around the Christmas season?

Sonya creatively reaches for God by asking Him for a word from the Bible for the next year. All during the month of December, she is alert, asking God to reveal a phrase, a verse, or a word that will help her connect to Him uniquely in the coming year. One year, her word was *trust*—and she did learn to trust in many different ways throughout the year. Trust informed the way she read Scripture, and God used that word to encourage her to continue to believe in His ways, even when life didn't seem to make sense. She pictured Peter trusting Christ as he stepped into the waves, and that picture sustained her. (see Matthew 14:22–33).

But our times of reflection in December shouldn't merely center around personal improvement. Sometimes we're so busy trying to re-create ourselves or micromanaging our own relationships with God that we forget He is the divine carver. Instead of worrying about whether you're good enough, or fretting about how you fall short, reorient your thinking. You are God's poem, His masterpiece. Trust in His artistic vision for you. Determine not to grab God's artist palette, but to trust that He sees beauty in you as no one else can. God is your skilled Sculptor, one who pursues your best, chipping away at the rough spots until freedom results.

While asking for a special word or phrase from the Bible involves reaching for Jesus in a creative way, simply being His masterpiece reflects the creativity He has expressed to you. And what's more creative than leaving the glory of heaven and coming into this world as a baby? People expected a king but received an infant. That infant grew up, lived a perfect life, then died so you could become His child, His masterpiece.

Let Jesus speak over you. Be still in order to hear His voice. And let Him have artistic license in your life, in this Christmas season, and in every day beyond.

Jesus, please whisper a word to me for next year, and help me to allow You to shape my heart in new ways. You are the sculptor; I am Your humble masterpiece—and for that I'm grateful. Amen.

Activity

Ask God for a word to focus on next year; then choose to create something around that word. Print it out and place it in a strategic place for the next year.

Let Jesus speak over you. Be still in order to hear His voice. And let Him have artistic license in your life, in this Christmas season, and in every day beyond.

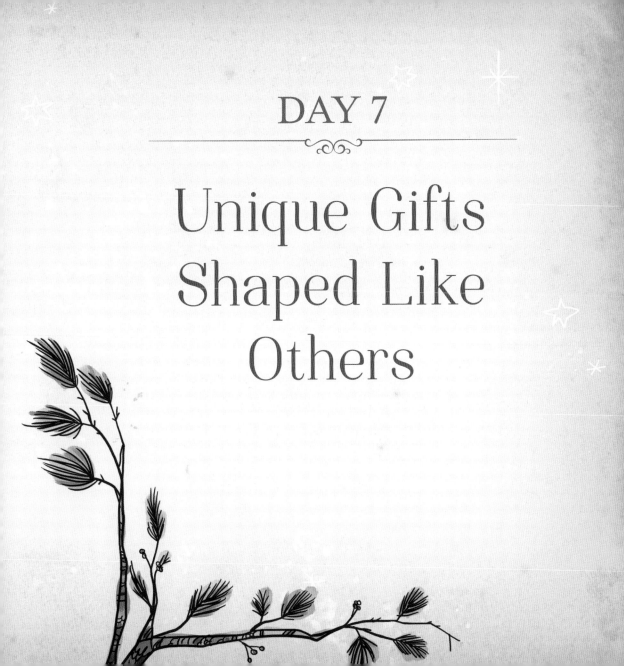

DAY 7

Unique Gifts Shaped Like Others

Be devoted to one another in love.

Honor one another above yourselves.

ROMANS 12:10

Rebecca sat in front of the tree, watching her children scamper around the pile of wrapping paper. Her husband winked at her, then handed her a present. "Merry Christmas," he said, with a Santa-like twinkle in his eye.

She pulled away the paper, wondering what his look meant. He knew she loved surprises. Was this one?

She opened the box and looked inside. Two airplane tickets and a brochure with the Eiffel Tower beaming from its cover. "Tomorrow," he said.

"Tomorrow?"

"Tomorrow we fly to Paris!"

Rebecca hugged her husband, laughter permeating the air. The children danced. She nearly cried. They were living on one income while he attended seminary, so this gift seemed especially extravagant. Only later did she find out he had thrifted his way through the gift planning, relinquishing airline points to make the trip entirely feasible.

They spent a week in Paris, walking the cold streets and falling in love with France. They shopped, ate, stayed in an amazing hotel, went to museums, and celebrated the New Year. They toasted the future.

Gifts are powerful, and they should spring from love and your unique relationship with the recipient. And because each person God places in our lives is a beautiful individual with quirks and affections and dislikes, we should strive to give gifts that deeply reflect that person's taste or needs. Rebecca's husband knew she needed an escape. He knew she loved France (always from afar). He knew her penchant for art museums and amazing food. So, he gave.

This type of meaningful giving reflects the way Jesus gives to you. He knows you intimately. He can meet you where you are and encourage you in ways that are shaped only like you. When you participate in purposeful giving, remember this truth: Jesus is a good gift giver, and He loves to give good gifts to His children.

The gifts you give others need not be extravagant. But they should reflect God's affection for the person to whom you're giving, an honoring of his or her unique contribution to the world. Give a gift that says, "I've noticed you. I've seen what you love"—a perfect reflection of Jesus' outrageous gift.

May we become mindful this season, purposeful and creative in the gifts we give others, never forgetting that Jesus is the original gift.

Lord, I want to honor those to whom I give gifts. Please help me know what will truly bless my loved ones this season. Is it the gift of time? A little something that will touch each of them? Please show me. And as You do, I want to remember that You are the great Giver of gifts. You have blessed me with so much, and You know just what to send my way when I struggle. Thank You, Jesus.

Activity

Spend the next week with your gift-alert system activated. Listen to what your family and friends say, how they hint. What do they truly need? Consider writing out prayers for a struggling friend in a new notebook to give to her. Or plan a surprise outing for a mom who needs a break.

> Because each person God places in our lives is a beautiful individual with quirks and affections and dislikes, we should strive to give gifts that deeply reflect that person's taste or needs.

DAY 8

Longing for *Home*

Jesus replied, "Foxes have dens and birds have nests,

but the Son of Man has no place to lay his head."

LUKE 9:58

After a difficult stint of missionary living overseas, Shannon and her family moved back to Texas a few days before Christmas. Things seemed overwhelming as they unpacked their few belongings in a small apartment in the corner of a horse barn.

They scraped together a Christmas by shopping in the crowded aisles of a large discount chain store. Actually, the better word is *survived*. Normally Shannon was the kind of person who was addicted to her to-do lists and had Christmas figured out in June, but with all the transition, she ended up becoming a last-minute shopper.

Shannon learned new things about homelessness that Christmas as she and her family lived in their temporary home. Though not homeless in the purest sense of the word, for a month they didn't live in a permanent place. In a similar way, Jesus didn't have a permanent place when He stooped low to earth to be born of Mary. He left His home, paradise, to dwell among us. Today's scripture reminds us that He had no place to even lay His head.

Shannon felt small living in that barn, but she also felt less frazzled. She learned to endure the transition as she longed for a permanent home. She understood afresh that Jesus endured times of having no permanent home for many years—when His parents were nomadic after His birth and during His ministry years—all for our sakes. She learned to love Him all the more because of it. He had walked where Shannon walked—in that netherworld of transition and vagabond ways.

Many of us experience transience like Shannon's, and in that transition, we feel untethered and alone. But like her, you too can experience a sense of home as you cling to the Savior who understands. Ponder these essential truths: God has empowered you to give and receive love. He has given you loved ones. And even if you find yourself alone this Christmas, you are never truly alone because you have Jesus. He is all you need, and He is your home.

You may not be living in a barn this Christmas, but you have a Savior who did. And He who often had no place to lay His head knows best how to bring joy no matter what circumstances you face.

Lord, You are my haven in the midst of transition—whatever form that may take. Bring me back to simplicity where I see what is truly important: You and the people You created around me. A home. Love. Life in the moment. And most importantly, help me to find my home in You. Amen.

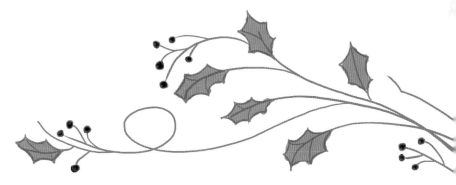

Activity

Search for a ministry in your area that seeks to bless refugees and newly arrived immigrants to the United States. Ask for tangible ways your family can bless a displaced family.

God has empowered you to give and receive love. He has given you loved ones. And even if you find yourself alone this Christmas, you are never truly alone because you have Jesus. He is all you need, and He is your home.

Embrace Your Stillness

"Be still, and know that I am God;

I will be exalted among the nations,

I will be exalted in the earth."

PSALM 46:10

Jackie had a hard time finding peace when the Christmas season knocked on the door of her life. Every year, she determined to do a better job of managing stress and slowing down. She remembered what she called "the ragged years," when her children were small, and she could scarcely get a night's sleep amid the chaos. She had always spent too much, regretting it when January's bills arrived. And each year when she looked back, she experienced the stinging pain of regret. In all her rushing, she had missed so many moments—time with people she should have cherished instead of rushing through the season, checking her watch.

This year would be different.

She began by memorizing Psalm 46:10, by printing it off and placing it on her car's dashboard. *Be still and know that He is God*, she reminded herself. As she settled into this truth, she realized she didn't have to be God. She certainly didn't have to be perfect. Her stillness allowed Him to be big while she felt small. And even when she made a holiday mistake, He would still be exalted in the world. Stillness replaced frenzy. Peace co-opted scurry. Jackie's Christmas became a time of reflective joy.

Another thing Jackie found as she meditated on this scripture was that Jesus showed up in the margins of her life. As she practiced stillness, choosing not to fret, He connected with her. When she heard Christmas carols, she reveled in the lyrics. Waiting in line, something that used to drive her batty, became a time to pray for her loved ones.

How about you? Has Christmas become an endless chore to be endured rather than cherished? Has the rush of the season stolen your joy? There must be a better way to move through the holidays—to be able to slow down and not get caught up in the rat race of preparation and overspending.

Connecting to God through stillness, through reminding yourself that He is God and you don't have to be, can create needed margin in your life. Slow down. Drink some hot chocolate in front of a fire. Read through the Gospel accounts of Jesus coming to earth. And as you do, pray for stillness, rest, and rejuvenation.

Be still and know that He is God . . .

Lord, help me to slow down and enjoy the holidays, especially as Christmas nears. I choose this day to rest, to savor, and to think about You. Amen.

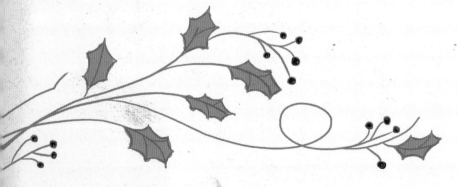

Activity

One of the great losses families have experienced is a connection with the outdoors, cutting themselves off from the natural world. Instead of staking claim to a big-box store, find adventure outside the box. Take walks in holiday-themed neighborhoods. Go ice skating. Sing Christmas carols to your neighbors. Feed the ducks at a local lake. You'll not only gain much-needed, stress-busting exercise, but you'll also bond as you experience God's creation together.

Connecting to God through stillness, through reminding yourself that He is God and you don't have to be, can create needed margin in your life.

DAY 10

Cheerful, Sacrificial Gifts

Each of you should give what you have decided in your

heart to give, not reluctantly or under compulsion,

for God loves a cheerful giver.

2 CORINTHIANS 9:7

G od had put Clara on Katie's mind. Every time Katie took a walk, God prompted Katie to pray for her friend. Whenever she had a quiet moment in the car, again God encouraged her to intercede. Initially Katie thought she'd let Clara know that God had been prompting her to pray, but then she sensed instead that God had something else in mind. Just two months before Christmas, He wanted Katie to handwrite her prayers, then give those prayers to Clara as a Christmas present.

So, Katie purchased a little journal and began to pour out her prayers on Clara's behalf. She prayed for Clara's heart, her marriage, her relationships with her children, and any sort of stress Katie thought Clara might be facing. She worried a little as she expressed these prayers in ink. Would they hit the mark? Were they the right prayers to pray? Still, she persisted, penning her prayers as God led her. Every night for two months, Katie refused to go to bed until she had written whatever it was that burdened her that day for Clara.

There were times when Katie's worries over the suitability of her words made her want to quit her journaling exercise. After all, Clara would never know. But about halfway through her reflection, she would remind herself of the truth of today's verse—that God wanted her to give purposefully, not with a grudge or a "have to." No, she would give joyfully. And as she continued to write her prayers, joy returned.

And then her joy magnified when she wrapped the journal, slipped it into a mailer, and sent it off in the mail.

When Clara unwrapped the gift, she cried. Speechless, she could not even call Katie because she feared the tears would interfere with her words. Katie's prayers had mirrored her depressive thoughts and feelings of hopelessness. Her worries had been carried to Jesus by Katie. Knowing God had prompted Katie to create this outrageous gift made Clara fall in love with Jesus all over again that Christmas.

This year's Christmas gifts don't have to cost money. Whatever you give is a mirror of Jesus' generosity. He, the maker of the universe, is wildly creative, wholly unexpected—and He gives joyfully. He surprises us daily with blessings.

He even gave Himself.

As you pray about the gifts you give family and friends, stop to think about God's creative abilities and His many surprising gifts to you. Then give—cheerfully.

Jesus, thank You for being an indescribable gift. Thanks for giving me my home, my family, and my life. Lord, help me to focus on Your extravagant giving as I seek for ways to bless my family and friends. Give me good ideas for gifts I can create. Amen.

Activity

Write out your prayers for a friend or family member for a period of two weeks to a month. Then give them that notebook as a gift.

This year's Christmas gifts don't have to cost money. Whatever you give is a mirror of Jesus' generosity.

Consider the Pebble

He gave up his divine privileges; he . . . was born as a

human being . . . He humbled himself.

Philippians 2:7–8 nlt

There is so much beauty in the commonplace, yet, we often chase after the shiny opportunities, content to exhaust ourselves for flash rather than find presence in the moment. We revere what is big, while despising what is small. In *Stone Crossings*, author L. L. Barkat laments:

> *Maybe, in a kind of selfish pride, I prefer the Master side of God better than the Child, so I look for the big ministry opportunities while neglecting hundreds of opportunities presented every day—in the fields of my common relationships.*

Barbara could relate. Always charitable, this year she had planned a large-scale, grandiose Christmas fund-raiser for charity. There would be media coverage and local celebrities to draw donors with deep pockets. *Just think of all the money we will raise!* she reasoned.

Then she saw a homeless man, obviously ill and wearing a thin, threadbare coat, and she almost passed right by him—until God spoke. Would she really put all of her time and energy into that spectacular, high-profile charity affair, yet ignore the thankless, very mundane task of reaching out to one whom Jesus would have considered "the least of these" (Matthew 25:31–46 NKJV)?

Perhaps you, too, prefer the spectacular to the mundane. But during this season of Advent, keep remembering God as a baby. Of all the ways that God could have announced Himself, He chose the humblest means. He who filled the universe with Himself . . . went small.

God reconfigured His majesty in the womb of a peasant. He stooped lower than we'll ever stoop. He, the Rock of Ages, became, in the quarry of His own making, a pebble, good only for paths underfoot.

While you may dream of doing big things for God this Christmas season, don't forget the unnoticed pebble, the humility, the stark reality of God becoming the holy child. In the greatest reversal of history, God traded opulence for ordinariness—for our sake.

In that musing, revisit Barkat's words. Then reflect on this: perhaps worshiping the baby in a manger has more to do with noticing who He places before us and loving them in ordinary, pedestrian ways. If God so lowered Himself to relate and commune with us, shouldn't we follow in His footsteps? To stoop? To empty? To open our eyes to the divine possibilities in our daily lives?

On your next walk, notice the boulder—then pick up a pebble. May that pebble serve as an object lesson of the greatness and humbleness of your God.

Lord, forgive me for trying to be grandiose, for forgetting the humility You portrayed by emptying Yourself of accolades. What a holy risk You took by becoming a pebble! Help me today to honor Your transformation by becoming part of Your redemptive plan. By loving those You place in my life in quiet, unheralded moments. Help me to pick up a pebble today and consider the enormity of what You've done. Help the weight of it in my pocket remind me to walk humbly and simply with You, being attuned to Your whispers, no matter what they say. Amen.

Activity

Have each person in your circle find a pebble, and then read today's devotion. Instruct them to place the rock in a strategic place (a dresser, near the mirror, etc.) as a reminder that the foundation of our faith became small in order to save us.

During this season of Advent, keep remembering God as a baby. Of all the ways that God could have announced Himself, He chose the humblest means. He who filled the universe with Himself . . . went small.

DAY 12

The Surprise Gift

"Look at the birds of the air; they do not sow or reap or store away in barns, and yet your heavenly Father feeds them. Are you not much more valuable than they?"

MATTHEW 6:26

Anna faced a difficult holiday in a new place. Her surroundings felt utterly unfamiliar. Even the stores were hard to navigate. Locating simple grocery items became a chore. Top that off with the fact that in her move, she'd left behind her mixer—a prized possession for a baker like herself. Everything would have to be stirred by hand this year.

A few days before Christmas, Reese, a friend of hers, called. "I had a dream," he told her.

"You were in your kitchen," he continued, "mixing, mixing, mixing. Flour, eggs, everything. I saw you throw up your hands, spatulas flying. Then I heard the word *mixer*. Does that mean anything to you?" His voice held laughter.

Anna remembered how she'd lamented in front of her friend about leaving her mixer behind. But he interrupted her thought.

"It's settled, then," he said. "I'm taking you shopping—for a mixer."

Reese took Anna and her family to the appliance store. The red, five-quart stand mixer she had admired on several occasions beckoned there. She gazed at it longingly.

"You want red?" he asked, noticing her stare.

"Yeah, but, it's really expensive."

"Please let me do this, Anna," said Reese. "I enjoy giving."

That night, Anna carried home a red mixer—a present of spectacular extravagance from the hands of Jesus through a generous and kind man.

When Anna looked at that gift, she smiled, knowing that Jesus loved her enough to take care of trivial matters, like missing a beloved appliance. He saw Anna. He watched over her. He knew her.

God's grace is extravagant, outlandish, surprising, and humbling like that. Anna's friend demonstrated that to her. But more than the tangible expression of God's love in the form of a mixer, we can thank Jesus for coming to earth, leaving the glory of heaven, and dwelling in our world. Because He did this outrageous act, He understands our trials. He sees our struggle. He identifies with our needs and wants and worries. We have a God who is well acquainted with our internal struggles, and He loves to meet us in them.

Lord, thank You for seeing me, even when I feel unnoticed. Thank You for loving me extravagantly, and for humbling Yourself so that I can understand what love is. Amen.

Activity

Choose a day next month when you will give a surprise, unmerited gift to someone you know who is struggling.

Jesus understands our trials. He sees our struggle. He identifies with our needs and wants and worries. We have a God who is well acquainted with our internal struggles, and He loves to meet us in them.

DAY 13

Sacred Rest

"Also I gave them my Sabbaths as a sign between us,

so they would know that I the Lord *made them holy."*

J eannie felt overworked and overwhelmed. During the holidays she faced all sorts of stress: financial, family, work, relational, personal, and spiritual. Instead of lessening her worries, Christmas seemed to augment her stress. She didn't have space to breathe or ponder or even plan. Instead, the season rushed past her, all while she rushed to keep up.

One Sunday, just before Thanksgiving, Jeannie's pastor reminded their small congregation about rest. He waxed poetic about the Sabbath, focusing on the need to slow down long enough to really reconnect with Jesus, particularly during the month we should be worshiping Him and celebrating His birth. He encouraged families to rethink what the Sabbath might look like for them.

Leading up to Christmas, Jeannie decided to make one day a week sacred. Not in some sort of legalistic, sit-in-a-chair-and-read-a-book way, but with a view toward freedom and joy.

On the Saturday before each Advent Sunday, Jeannie prepared for rest by doing her food prep so the next day wouldn't be all about the kitchen. Sometimes her family decided in advance to go out on Sunday to keep the kitchen clean. Other times she used paper plates and disposable utensils to keep work to a minimum. Planning this way made for relaxing Sundays, and it gave her the space she needed to reflect.

Jeannie realized that creating something of beauty had the huge potential to rejuvenate her, so she gave herself permission to paint—something she'd always loved to do but seldom made time for. Her family also ventured outside, taking walks through the nearby woods, breathing deeply, and slowing down. One Sunday evening, her husband built a fire in a fire pit. They sang Christmas songs in the hush of night, drank hot chocolate, and ate s'mores with peppermint-flavored marshmallows. Suddenly, the pandemonium of the Christmas season, with all of its fuss and frenzy and to-do lists, gave way to peace.

How about you? Has this season typically become one of frenetic activity? Why not take a day off? When you do, you'll feel refreshed, alive, new, and ready for the week. With the rush of life, could you orchestrate some holy rhythm this weekend? To create the white space needed to be thankful? To find retreat within the four walls of your home? To do things in worship that rejuvenate your soul?

Let this end-of-the-year season be full of sacred, restful moments like this, where you pull away from hassle, reconnect with your friends and family, and seek to truly retreat. In the hurry of the holidays, folks tend to expend a lot of energy. Setting aside one day a week will rejuvenate you all year long, and taking a week or two off after Christmas will give you the jump start you need for the year to come.

Jesus, I'm tired. Help me to stop a moment to rest and rejuvenate. Help me include rest in my life every week, time to pull away and renew. And during this vacation, Lord, I pray You would help me truly, deeply rest. Amen.

Activity

During your time of rest, write down what worked well last year and what could be improved. Use this brainstorming session as a point of prayer for the things you'd like to do differently next year. Be sure to include rest as a viable part of next year.

Let this end-of-the-year season be full of sacred, restful moments where you pull away from hassle, reconnect with your friends and family, and seek to truly retreat.

The Art of
Contentment

Jesus looked at him and loved him. "One thing you lack,"

he said. "Go, sell everything you have and give to the

poor, and you will have treasure in heaven. Then come,

follow me." At this the man's face fell. He went away sad,

because he had great wealth.

MARK 10:21–22

Christmastime had a way of making Macy feel smaller. It cemented what she already felt about herself—that she wasn't enough, particularly because she didn't have all the things she longed for. Even though she knew deep down that her worth wasn't the same as her bottom line, living amid the sparkle of department stores and seemingly unlimited Internet ads made her feel "less than."

It wasn't until she volunteered to drive shoe boxes filled with gifts to one of the poorest neighborhoods in Mexico that she realized how far her heart had strayed from the truth: that Jesus loved her for who she was, not what she owned. When the young children she encountered received the simple gifts of toothbrushes, dime-store toys, and soccer balls, she noted their joy. And as she ventured into their homes, noticing how their meager possessions didn't diminish their joy (they actually rejoiced more than the kids she'd seen in her affluent suburb), she knew something needed to change, and it had nothing to do with money or stuff.

When she returned to her home state, she determined to be grateful for what she had. She began writing in a gratitude journal. As she did, something beautiful happened in her heart. She realized that Jesus loved her for her, not for what she had, and that her value as a person truly had nothing to do what whatever stuff she owned. In that, she learned the art of contentment.

Have you struggled with your worth? Have you, like Macy, allowed the world's vision of happiness (having more stuff) to influence your joy? Instead of making lists of things you think you want this Christmas, make it a new habit to list the things and people you're thankful for. That

Christmas list will help you remember that your life is more than stuff, and your worth is securely connected to Jesus' affection for you. Oh, how He loves His children!

Dear Jesus, I need contentment, and I need You to remind me to be satisfied with what I have. As I list the things and people I'm thankful for, would You meet me in that sacred space? Forgive me for thinking I'll be happy if I just get more things. I am so grateful that Your love for me isn't tied at all to my bottom line. Your bottom line is simply this: You love me. And that is enough. Amen.

Activity

Grab a piece of paper and list all the things and people you are grateful for. Place that list in your Bible to remind you of the beautiful truth that you are more than things, and that your true joy lies in staying connected to Jesus, the source of all gifts.

Instead of making lists of things you think you want this Christmas, make it a new habit to list the things and people you're thankful for.

Good Gifts and Worth

This is how God showed his love among us:

He sent his one and only Son into the world that we

might live through him. This is love: not that we loved

God, but that he loved us and sent his Son as an

atoning sacrifice for our sins.

1 JOHN 4:9–10

odie hated going to the store during the holidays. Oh, she hated shopping anyway, but during the Christmas rush her stress rose exponentially. Why? Because she had a hard time spending money during lean times, and she worried all the time that she wouldn't have enough money for the month.

But beyond that, Jodie felt *she* didn't deserve good things. While she might be able to justify spending money on a much-anticipated doll for her granddaughter (to her this was a worthy sacrifice), when it came to herself, she had an internal struggle. One afternoon in the grocery store stood out. After debating the merits of candy canes, she stood in front of the dryer sheets and wondered if she should purchase them.

I don't deserve these, she thought to herself. *But it would be nice to have some.* She checked the price of a well-known brand. Back and forth she debated with herself, finally deciding that she could buy some, but only the store brand. She felt she didn't deserve the more expensive brand.

Have you ever felt like this? That you don't deserve good gifts? You may be able to lavishly give to those you love, even sacrificing as Jodie did, but when it comes to you, you have a hard time receiving. And maybe sometimes you push others away or constantly deny yourself because deep down you don't feel worthy.

The truth is this: you are so deeply loved! Jesus loves you. And He gives you good gifts. You may not fret over a purchase so small, but you may have had a similar store conversation with God. Perhaps you had an inclination that you don't deserve a small splurge, or you had the feeling that

God wouldn't gift you with a sweet surprise. And yet we read in the verse above that God loves us so much that He sent His Son as a sacrifice for us.

Settle into that truth today, particularly as you prepare to celebrate the greatest gift of all time—God's gift of His Son for all of humanity. That's certainly an indescribable gift, and it represents the lengths God went to in making us right with Him. You are valued. You are sacrificed for. You are loved. You are beloved. Rest there.

Dear Jesus, sometimes I struggle with being blessed or allowing others to bless me. Sometimes my worth is so small in my own eyes that I can't accept Your extravagant gifts. Help me receive today. I open my hands and my heart. Amen.

Activity

Be on the lookout for Christian songs (and Christmas songs) that sing about our worth (like *O Holy Night*, which talks about when Christ "appear'd and the *soul felt its worth* / A thrill of hope the weary world rejoices / For yonder breaks a new and glorious morn!"). Create a playlist of these songs to immerse yourself in when you're battling with receiving from others or feeling small and unworthy.

The truth is this: you are so deeply loved! Jesus loves you. And He gives you good gifts. . . . Settle into that truth today, particularly as you prepare to celebrate the greatest gift of all time—God's gift of His Son for all of humanity.

DAY 16

You Are His Child

Yet to all who did receive him, to those who believed in

his name, he gave the right to become children of God—

children born not of natural descent, nor of human

decision or a husband's will, but born of God.

JOHN 1:12–13

Julia had a hole in her life that she couldn't quite fill. Although she desperately loved her adoptive parents, she had an insatiable desire to know where she came from and who had carried her for nine months. Around Christmastime, this need to know became acute.

Knowing this, her husband searched for her birth mother, only to discover the sad news that Julia's mom had passed away a decade earlier. This was not the news his wife had longed for, and it would not make a good Christmas gift. So he broke the news to her gently, then decided to try something else.

That Christmas, he gave her a different kind of gift—a DNA kit so she could discover her heritage in a different way. She loved it! She immediately swabbed her cheek, then awaited her results. Her hands shook as she opened the envelope. She read, tears streaming down her face. Suddenly, many of her traits made sense. Knowing her ethnicity and background helped her finally understand things about herself.

But after she read everything, she remembered something more: no matter who she was or whose she was, the truth remained that she would always be a child of God. He knew all along what her journey would be. He chose her adoptive parents and her birth parents. He had led her gently through her life, teaching her, encouraging her, disciplining her as a good father would. While it was a joy to know more about her background, a deeper joy flooded through her. All along, she had been God's child, dearly loved, watched over, and sung over.

Today's scripture reminds us that we are children of God. It is a right and privilege bought with the precious blood of Jesus Christ. Because He left eternity and humbled Himself to be born a baby, lived a perfect life, then sacrificed Himself on the cross, you can now live the privileged life as an adopted child of God.

Dear Jesus, I'm so grateful that You have secured my place in Your family. When I begin to fret over my position here on earth, remind me again that I am Your child. This is secure, a known truth. When I feel far from You, remind me that my feelings don't dictate what is the truth—that I am Yours. Amen.

Activity

Find a tangible way to bless an orphan this Christmas. Ministries such as Compassion International actively help orphans—seek to give toward that end. Or perhaps there's a local children's home that needs more supplies, and your family could provide some much-needed resources. Whatever you do, be a blessing to someone who needs to know that he or she is God's child.

We are children of God. It is a right and a privilege bought with the precious blood of Jesus Christ.

How Well Do You Love Those Who Differ?

My dear brothers and sisters, take note of this:

Everyone should be quick to listen, slow to speak and

slow to become angry, because human anger does not

produce the righteousness that God desires.

JAMES 1:19–20

Jesus spent time with people who had vastly different lifestyles from those considered "holy" in His day. Tax collectors and sinners flocked to Him. He invited them near and welcomed them into His circle. He was not afraid of other people's opinions. He always spoke the truth, but seasoned it with grace. He reserved His harshest, most critical words for those who appeared religious but were hypocritical. He was so inviting to the masses that thousands followed Him.

Marcia has recently learned to be more like Jesus. In past years at Christmas dinner, she'd taken special pleasure in starting a political argument with her brother-in-law, who had voted for the other candidate in the last presidential election. She'd bickered with her son because she disagreed with his lifestyle. She'd even quibbled with her sister about how much sage should be in the dressing. She had little tolerance for those who had opinions different from hers, and she quickly became angry.

Today, though, thanks to Jesus' gentle voice, Marcia is a wellspring of joy to her family, especially during the holidays. Her smile lights up a room. She defuses condemning conversations. And her nieces and nephews can't wait to spend Christmas with Aunt Marcia.

How do we represent this irresistibility of Jesus during this Advent season when we interact with people who differ from us—sometimes around our holiday table? Would Jesus yell at someone who differed in her political opinion? Would He lash out and demean her? Would He scream? Do hollering and pouting and stirring up fear represent Jesus' manner of doing things?

Consider this wisdom from Proverbs, remembering that Jesus is wisdom personified: "Fools give full vent to their rage, but the wise bring calm in the end" (29:11).

We are more like Jesus when we hold our tempers, when we choose not to stir up strife for the sake of proving our "correctness." Our job is not to convince others of their wrongness and our rightness. It's not to change people's hearts. (Only God can change a heart.) Our job is to represent Jesus, how He talked, how He acted, and how He loved.

If you struggle with this, ask yourself: Do I truly believe God is in control? If I do, then why all the anger? Other people's opinions cannot dethrone the beauty and power of God. He doesn't need us to manage His reputation. Consider that Jesus, being perfect, differed from every single human being He interacted with. And yet, He loved. He accepted people where they were. Their healing was not dependent on their properly held views.

The litmus test is this: How well do you love those who differ from you? God will not hold us accountable as much for our "correct" opinions or fervor as He'll call us to account for the way we love those who hold different views.

Dear Jesus, help me be so settled in Your love for me that very little threatens me or pushes me toward anger. I entrust myself to You. I want to be gentle, quick to listen, and slow to speak. Help me not be threatened by others' opinions. In the heat of disagreement, give me Your perspective and help me love those who differ. Amen.

Activity

Review the list of people you'll see over Christmas. Pray about your interactions with them ahead of time. Identify those whose opinions differ from yours, and brainstorm ways to defuse any potential anger. This kind of prep work will serve you well when you're in the midst of a discussion.

We are more like Jesus when we hold our tempers. . . . Our job is to represent Jesus, how He talked, how He acted, and how He loved.

DAY 18

Your Life's Garden

There is a time for everything . . .

a time to plant and a time to uproot.

ECCLESIASTES 3:1–2

Have you ever considered how beautiful the garden of Eden must have been? And to think, no weeds!

Evaluating your relationships as the year comes to an end, consider that, perhaps, some relationships are like weeds. Left unattended, they can overtake your life—not just physically, but emotionally too: they take up space in your mind. Such people have the potential to influence your day-to-day activities. Perhaps they have spoken destructive, painful words over your life. If you let these mean-spirited words take up residence in your mind as you mull them over and ruminate on what you could have possibly done to change people's minds about you, you'll lose your joy.

Ashley dreaded spending another Christmas with her cousin Simone. Simone always found some reason to criticize Ashley, whether it was her clothes, her children, or her work. Her words to Ashley were a constant source of pain as Ashley ran through them over and over in her mind throughout the year. She needed to find a way to move past it.

So how can you let go—particularly around the holidays, when you, like Ashley, will most likely have to interact with some of these folks? You can simply pretend the weeds are pretty, then tolerate and even water them. Many of us try desperately to hope for the best in the midst of painful relationships, jumping through hoops so all will be well. The result? The "weeds" threaten to take over our hearts and choke our resolve.

Another thing you can do is spray verbal toxic chemicals on them. This happens during direct confrontations. If you allow someone to hurt you to the point that you retaliate with angry, in-the-moment words, then you've given in to sin. Better to take the pain to Jesus and ask Him to be Your defender.

Ecclesiastes reminds us that there's a time to plant *and* a time to uproot. The healthy way to deal with difficult people is to ask the master gardener to fully uproot the weeds from your heart and mind. Sometimes this means a severing of relationship. Other times it means creating better boundaries that give you space to heal. Still other times, God restores the relationships in surprising ways. The point is, when God addresses your difficult relationships, healing begins. You simply can't be a beautiful, lush garden with noxious weeds constantly invading. The hard part? Sometimes weeds pose as flowers. And sometimes flowers look like weeds. Only the master gardener knows the difference and can order your life and relationships accordingly. The key to knowing what to do is staying close to the master gardener.

This Christmas would be an excellent time to entrust every relationship you have to the Lord, particularly the ones that drain you or tear you down. Evaluate your life right now. Which relationships might you need to water and nurture like flowers. Conversely, who are the weeds in your life? Who are you afraid to let go of? Who has acted like an enemy, speaking words of discouragement over you? Ask God for wisdom about what to do, and how to process your grief. As you face a new year with new relationships as well as old, place those difficult relationships in His capable hands. He will help you.

Dear Jesus, I know You're the master gardener. I trust You to pull the weeds that need to be pulled, and plant the flowers that need to be planted in my life's garden. Help me trust Your pruning and weeding. Amen.

Activity

Print off and color a summer coloring picture to bring it to life as winter closes in. Bring vibrancy to each flower and tree. As you color in the garden, pray for the people in your life who represent weedy relationships and ask God to do the miraculous in and through those relationships.

> Sometimes weeds pose as flowers. And sometimes flowers look like weeds. Only the master gardener knows the difference and can order your life and relationships accordingly. The key to knowing what to do is staying close to the master gardener.

Remember Who You Are

"Do not be afraid, you who are highly esteemed,"

[the angel] said. "Peace! Be strong now; be strong."

When he spoke to me, I was strengthened and said,

"Speak, my lord, since you have given me strength."

DANIEL 10:19

For some, these words of Daniel's are hard to read. *Highly esteemed*? *Be strong*? Although we know that throughout history God gave courage to people when they needed it, and He strengthened those who were weak, we sometimes forget that those same promises are for us. Why? Because we only see His love and care for other people.

Oh, Jesus loves that *person, but He surely can't love me!*

Denice had felt precisely that way, until her pastor and a loving church family had shown her how much she meant to Jesus. *I'm not pretty like my sister. I don't make as much money as my friends. My house is small. My past is so shameful. God couldn't love me.* Thankfully, over time she became stronger in the Lord.

Isn't it interesting how we can readily believe God's love toward other people but cannot accept it for ourselves? Why is that? Perhaps it's because we know ourselves. We are well acquainted with our failures and pitfalls. We know our penchant for sin. We don't look back on our lives with pride; instead, we fret over whether people will find us out and call us imposters. We know the warts and the unlovely parts of ourselves. Surely God sees all this too, right? Why would He choose to love us?

Yes, it is true that Jesus loves other people. But it's equally true that He completely, ardently loves you. Settling into that truth will revolutionize your life. As you prepare to celebrate Jesus in the manger, remember this: He made that journey from heaven to a sin-scarred earth to demonstrate His love for *you*, His dearly loved child. He lived a perfect life in obedience to His Father in order to be an acceptable sacrifice for your sins. He died on the cross and was resurrected on your behalf. Therefore, remember these truths:

You are not a person devalued by others' casual opinions.

You are not the sum of your righteous (or unrighteous) acts.

You are not a thing to be used.

You are not small and unworthy.

You are not insignificant.

You are not unlovely.

You are not deserving of deceit.

You are not the words spoken over you by unkind people.

You are not what they say you are.

No, you are who the Word says you are. Beloved. Welcomed. Cherished. Beautifully rejuvenated. Whole.

That's who you are. Like Daniel, you are deeply loved by God. Do you believe it today? It's true. Be at peace. Be strong. Be encouraged. Let go of the destructive words inside so you can hear the reality of God's tender, affectionate voice.

Dear Jesus, speak life over me. Help me to hear Your affirming whispers over me, Your words of courage and power and love and acceptance and grace. I need Your voice. Forgive me for letting other voices rule my mind and emotions. Help me to feel Your favor and to rest in Your pleasure right now. Amen.

Activity

Make a copy of today's devotional, enclose it in a card, and send it to a person you know who struggles with low self-esteem. Remind this friend that she is dearly loved by God, and that as a child of God, she is considered worthy.

As you prepare to celebrate Jesus in the manger, remember this: He made that journey from heaven to a sin-scarred earth to demonstrate His love for *you*, His dearly loved child.

DAY 20

The Worry Monster

"Therefore I tell you, do not worry about your life, what you will eat

or drink; or about your body, what you will wear. Is not life more than

food, and the body more than clothes? Look at the birds of the air;

they do not sow or reap or store away in barns, and yet your heavenly

Father feeds them. Are you not much more valuable than they?

Can any one of you by worrying add a single hour to your life?"

MATTHEW 6:25–27

Worry infuses our lives, and when we let it in, it takes over and makes a home inside us. As you enter the end-of-the-year chaos, remember that you have the ability to let go of worry, creating a haven in your life, insulated from the cares of this world. How can you do that this Christmas when pressures threaten to steal your joy?

Belinda knows the answer. She used to worry about her house not being decorated up to Martha Stewart's standards, about her children possibly being disappointed in her gifts to them, and about her cantankerous father coming to Christmas dinner. But now she calms herself every morning by reading a devotional and some Scripture to keep things in proper perspective. She lets the peace of the Lord come into her heart before she dives into her day.

When anxieties mount, grab your Bible and read carefully and prayerfully through Psalm 27. Remind yourself that God is your light. He is your fortress. He hides you from strife. He hears when you call on Him. He will not abandon you. Instead of worrying, wait for Him. This psalm is a powerful weapon against worry; it will sustain you in the middle of the night when worry has awakened you.

If worry is stealing your joy, tell someone. There is power in community. Galatians 6:2 reminds us to "bear one another's burdens, and so fulfill the law of Christ" (NKJV). When you keep things bottled up, they fester. When you share your stress, it dissipates. When you pray about it with someone else, your anxieties will flee.

But maybe there's something deeper at work. During a quiet moment this Christmas, ask yourself hard questions and journal your answers. Do you love worry more than you love God? Has worry become your comfort zone? Is it your automatic response? What do you gain by being full of worry? Why do you keep worrying? Working through your answers may surprise you, and your wrestling and wrangling with worry may open up new spaces in your heart to trust Jesus.

Remember: you can't add anything of value to your life by worrying. As Jesus reminds us in today's scripture, you can't elongate your life by worrying about it. Instead, take this moment to surrender your stress to Jesus. He understands. He already knows what you need.

Jesus, I'm so tired of worrying. I need a new perspective on my life, one that doesn't include constant worry. Free me from this monster! Keep me so close to You that I feel safe and secure. Amen.

Activity

Write down every worry you have right now, one per small piece of paper. Fold them, then put them in a Mason jar. Place that jar in a cupboard and ask Jesus to take your worries. Next month, revisit what you wrote down and reflect on God's ability to help you in the midst of worry.

Worry infuses our lives, and when we let it in, it takes over and makes a home inside us. As you enter the end-of-the-year chaos, remember that you have the ability to let go of worry, creating a haven in your life, insulated from the cares of this world.

The Best Christmas Light

And God said, "Let there be light,"

and there was light.

GENESIS 1:3

T oday's verse records four amazing words God spoke: *Let. There. Be. Light.*

God loves light. He is light. He created it first, before anything else that exists. This light scattered and shattered the darkness. Knowing that central truth will help you appreciate all the lights you see during Christmas even more. Darkness simply cannot remain dark when a light appears! Even Jesus' birth was announced through a great light (star) in the sky (see Matthew 2:1–2)!

In a very real way, light and truth are intertwined. The God of light wants His children to live in the light, to speak and inhabit truth, to run away from that which holds us in darkness, particularly devastating secrets.

So why do we sometimes spend our lives hiding in the dark? Why do we prefer keeping secrets to the freedom of letting it all out? Jesus says these pointed words in John 3:19: "This is the verdict: Light has come into the world, but people loved darkness instead of light because their deeds were evil."

It doesn't make sense, does it? Why would we prefer secretive darkness more than light and truth and freedom? If we do stay in the shadows, it's an indication that a part of us loves darkness more. And that desire to stay in the dark comes from fear. Fear that if we tell the truth, we'll lose relationship. Fear that we'll forfeit our positions or reputations. Fear that we'll suffer under the judgment of others. Fear of simply not knowing how to live in the light because when you live in the dark most of your life, the light is terrifying.

Many find familiarity in the darkness. We wrongly think we are "worth" the darkness. The voice in your head yells your un-worth so loudly and so often that you have truly believed it, perhaps for many years. "Oh yeah," people might have said. "You really are worthless." Except that the people who love you *didn't* say that. "I have felt the same way," they may have told you. "But you're worth so much more."

Those are words for you today. Has darkness become your companion? Do you often listen to the shout of un-worth in your head? Do you believe it? Has living this way become easy and convenient? Does the thought of coming to the light terrify you?

It need not terrify, because Jesus is that Light. Remember Him, how He loved people, how He welcomed them despite their scary secrets. He came to set us free, to render the devil (who lives in darkness 24/7) impotent, and to silence lies with light-filled truth. Step out into the light. Dare, today, to share one small segment of your darkness with a friend, and ask him or her to pray with you. That's what Dolly did. In her despair, she called a friend and poured out her heart to her, allowing her friend to pray with her and to dispel the darkness.

If you're feeling caught in the darkness this Christmas, do what Dolly did and reach out for help. You'll be surprised how much you'll begin to revel in the light, dancing free.

Jesus, You are light. Forgive me if I've preferred darkness and lies to Your light and truth. Speak worth over me. Free me from the thoughts I think in the darkness. Oh, how I need You. Amen.

Activity

Light a candle tonight in a dark room. Notice how it dissipates the darkness. Remember that when Jesus entered this darkened planet, He was the Light of the World.

In a very real way, light and truth are intertwined. The God of light wants His children to live in the light, to speak and inhabit truth, to run away from that which holds us in darkness, particularly devastating secrets.

DAY 22

Good for You

You intended to harm me, but God intended

it for good to accomplish what is now being done,

the saving of many lives.

GENESIS 50:20

What is the context of these powerful words? Joseph, who was sold into slavery by his own brothers, became a high leader in Egypt, responsible for saving the lives of many during the famine. He simply spoke the truth to his brothers: "Yes, you meant to hurt me, but in the long run, God can use even your evil actions and intentions to save many."

Yes, there may be some people from your past who did bad things to you or spoke harsh words over your life. Like Joseph's brothers, they may have meant evil against you. But after much, much healing, God will use your past devastation to help you help others who go through similar devastation. And He longs to set you free this Christmas.

There is more to Joseph's story than his pain becoming an avenue to rescue others. In Genesis 45:8, Joseph tells his brothers, "So then, it was not you who sent me here, but God." This is not an easy scripture to digest. Did God "send" you into the clutches of the very people who hurt you? Or did He send them to you? No, God's heart breaks when His children are defiled, so in both cases, this kind of logic won't work. However, if you look at it from a different perspective, you may find comfort.

God did send Jesus to earth to destroy the works of the evil one, but He did not send the evil one *after* His Son, or after Joseph. So, his point was not that God sends evil. Evil exists. What Joseph was revealing here is that people who do evil things are not themselves God. They cannot intersect time and eternity as Jesus did when He was born. Enemies may think they are destroying us, but the final outcome rests in God's hands. People don't have the ultimate power to change a life.

In other words, a perpetrator cannot thwart God's good plan for you. Although it's hard to understand the whys of the past, we must understand that God has a larger purpose in all this pain. You are now able to love those who have similar stories and empathize in ways you wouldn't have been able to had you not walked through what you experienced. You will have the privilege of telling someone who is in the same situation, "You are not alone, and you are not crazy."

Kathryn had experienced great trauma. Molested as a child, she had suffered with fear and distrust for years. But when she met Jesus, and He healed her heart, she began to turn her terror into a testimony, helping countless others like her to find peace and freedom.

As human beings, we cannot know why bad things happen. But you can tell your own story of redemption this Christmas because God has taken your hand on this journey and empowered you to help others be set gloriously free.

Jesus, please give me a new perspective on Your goodness in the midst of what happened to me back then. Remind me that even though those people in my past meant to hurt me, Your plan cannot be thwarted in my life. I pray for divine appointments this Christmas so I can share Your story of redemption in my life. Amen.

Activity

Write a letter to someone who has deeply wounded you. As God leads, choose to forgive that person. Don't mail the letter unless you sense you're supposed to. This is a cathartic exercise.

A perpetrator cannot thwart God's good plan for you. Although it's hard to understand the whys of the past, we must understand that God has a larger purpose in all this pain.

DAY 23

Sufficient

But he said to me, "My grace is sufficient for you, for my power is made perfect in weakness." Therefore I will boast all the more gladly about my weaknesses, so that Christ's power may rest on me. That is why, for Christ's sake, I delight in weaknesses, in insults, in hardships, in persecutions, in difficulties. For when I am weak, then I am strong.

2 CORINTHIANS 12:9–10

God is counterintuitive. His power is disguised as weakness.

Look at the way He chose to save His children—not through a military act or even another walk through the Red Sea. With everything at His disposal, His method wasn't a display of force but a surprising act of humbleness. He came from a manger, not a chariot, to save us.

And yet, we often think that to serve Him, we must expand ourselves, make ourselves important and large and great. How odd that we climb platforms as high as the tower of Babel, when He is the one who should be lifted high. We praise the able, applaud the winner, herald the hero. No wonder some of the Jewish people missed their Messiah. He wasn't what they expected. He didn't match what they thought a king should be.

Marilyn enjoyed ushering at her church, but when the pastor called for people to join the mission trip to India, she felt she should volunteer for that as well. Despite not feeling God calling her to India, she wanted to do something that would increase her stature with Him, and she thought the overseas trip would be just the thing. Sadly, she missed the fact that God already loves her more than she can imagine.

Propping ourselves up won't endear us to our humble Savior. Instead, learning what it means to identify with Him in our weakness will connect us to Him. When we do this, we acknowledge that He is God, and we are not. We display our understanding of His counterintuitive ways. What is strong is actually weak. What is weak is actually strong, when that weakness is married to His strength.

The "enoughness" of God is enough for you, no matter where you find yourself today. Give Him your striving to make things happen, instead entrusting Him to grow the tiny seed of your trust and dependence into something tree-like, planted by a deep riverbed. God causes the growth. God gets the glory when we realize it's all Him.

Apart from Jesus, you can do nothing. Nothing. Not a thing. (See John 15:5.) So, quit striving to succeed on your own. Quit believing that God only uses those other, "successful" folks for His kingdom. It's simply not true. He notices faithfulness, those prayers you cry out in the wee hours of the morning. He sees your dreams for His kingdom, those counterintuitive, God-sized dreams, and He longs to bring them to fruition.

But, just as at the first Christmas, He seldom follows our timetable or does things the way we expect Him to.

We need to let God be creative in our midst. He may have done things one way ten years ago, but if we make "that way" a hard-and-fast method or an expectation, we hinder the work of our Creator. Let God be new. Let God innovate. Let Him take the reins (in other words, let Him reign).

Jesus, help me realize that I don't have to strive after success and flash to be used by You. I'm grateful for Your simple example of coming to earth in a manger. Help me stay in that simple, trusting place. Amen.

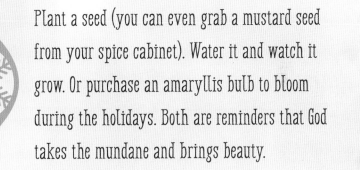

Activity

Plant a seed (you can even grab a mustard seed from your spice cabinet). Water it and watch it grow. Or purchase an amaryllis bulb to bloom during the holidays. Both are reminders that God takes the mundane and brings beauty.

With everything at Jesus' disposal, His method wasn't a display of force, but a surprising act of humbleness. He came from a manger, not a chariot, to save us.

DAY 24

Giving Joyfully from the Heart

"If you, then, though you are evil, know how to give good

gifts to your children, how much more will your Father

in heaven give good gifts to those who ask him!"

MATTHEW 7:11

Ever since Haven was a little girl, she fretted about giving gifts. Maybe because she loved receiving them so much, she feared that the gift she would give would not make the person receiving it happy. This paralyzed Haven—this worry that her gift wouldn't be good enough or important enough. When she had little money, she would make gifts for others. As a teen, she created handmade books, full of quotes and ideas and art that she tailor-made for each recipient. You can imagine the relief she felt when those gifts hit the mark, and her family members appreciated them with tears.

But oh, the gift stress!

You'd think by now Haven would be a confident gift giver. But as she got older and busier, there were many times when the gifts she gave weren't the right fit, mostly because she was simply filling a slot on a gift list rather than spending a lot of time placing herself in the person's shoes and uncovering what would make him or her truly happy. In other words, when gift giving became rote and unemotional, it wasn't very successful.

Eventually, after studying the life of Jesus more extensively, Haven learned to let go of all these stressful expectations, particularly around Christmas. Noticing how Jesus focused on the unique needs of the person in front of Him, Haven grasped the importance of simply giving, always with the person in mind. This new perspective freed her from all the have-tos and you-shoulds. It gave her permission to give joyfully from the heart, not to fill a slot, but to bless a person.

Now Haven remembers that gift giving is a reflection of all Jesus has done for her. By coming to earth and living a very human life full of pain and everyday struggles, He gave her (and you!) the greatest gift of all—Himself. His radical obedience to die on a cross for our sins means all of us have unfettered access to the Father. We can walk around whole and healed because of His forgiveness that came through His death and resurrection. What an indescribably beautiful gift! All other gifts pale by comparison.

The gift Jesus gives requires involvement, and it reflects sacrifice. Perhaps there are people in your life who can benefit from either. Each day you have the unique opportunity to see things from other people's perspectives. Instead of judging immediately, remember how Jesus listened to people and explored their needs. As you put yourself in other people's shoes, this will not only increase your empathy, but it will empower you as you strive to give meaningful gifts.

Jesus, keep me mindful of the needs of the people around me. I don't want gift giving to be stressful. Instead, I want my gifts, whether tangible or intangible, to represent You, the greatest gift of all. Amen.

Activity

Make extra dinner tonight and deliver it to someone who may need it. Enclose a card with a prayer for that person.

The gift Jesus gives requires involvement, and it reflects sacrifice. Perhaps there are people in your life who can benefit from either.

Find the Joy of Christmas in the Darkness

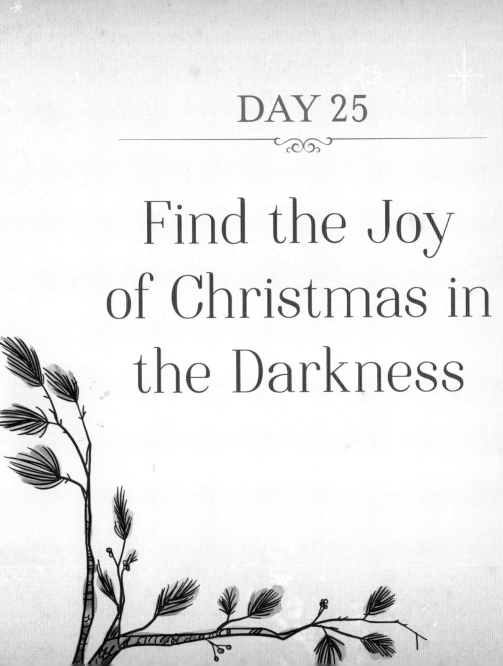

"But when you are praying, first forgive anyone

you are holding a grudge against, so that your

Father in heaven will forgive your sins, too."

MARK 11:25 NLT

Jean and her brother David hadn't spoken in years, and it was all because of a falling out over some property in their mother's estate. This year David would be coming to Christmas dinner, and Jean just prayed for peace.

Christmas is typically full of relationships—friends, coworkers, and family members spending more time together. Family gathers from long distances to celebrate. While this represents sheer joy for some—a bright spot in the midst of a dark winter—for others, broken relationships bring heavy darkness.

Why? Maybe someone's actions sent you into a place you never intended to be. Perhaps you have to bear the cost of someone else's sin against you, and you'll be seeing that person during the holidays.

It would be great if we lived in a world where friends and family members and spouses acted becomingly all the time—especially during festive celebrations. (And if we would act that way as well.) But unfortunately, we don't, and people's actions can cause us such pain that we feel isolated and joyless.

What are we to do in this dark place? How can we move on? Is it possible to have joy in our celebrations even when other people's decisions hurt us?

God gives us a choice. We can choose to flourish. This begins by a simple but painful decision to forgive, and it continues by trusting God for outcomes. We can either give in to bitterness, nursing it, justifying it, letting it prevent abundance, or we can take a courageous leap to live differently. Yes, it hurt. Yes, the betrayal happened.

But it's equally true that Jesus experienced the same betrayal. Family members and friends hurt Him. And because He walked through similar pain, He can come alongside you. He empathizes with you, loves you, and wants to help you find victory in the midst of pain. That's why James tells us to consider it pure joy when trials come (James 1:2). It's why Jeremiah encouraged the nation of Israel to "work for the peace and prosperity of the city" where they were sent into exile. "Pray to the Lord for it," he wrote, "for its welfare will determine your welfare" (Jeremiah 29:7 NLT).

Work to bring peace and prosperity wherever you are—even in dysfunctional family gatherings over the holidays. Choose to bloom where you've been planted, even if the planting is not your choice. God promises strength when you are weak, perspective when you're sad or despondent, and love when you feel unloved.

The truth is, you can flourish. Someone else's mean choices do not impact your own choices. Rest in the embrace of Jesus, who understands being hurt. If you're bewildered, ask for His help. He loves to come to the aid of those who truly, deeply need Him. And perhaps that's the greatest gift of being hurt. When we're in that helpless place, we must rely on Him for strength. We must need Him, not our own solutions or vengeance. And when we walk in forgiveness, depending on Jesus, He brings light into those dark relationships.

Lord Jesus, I've been hurt. I'm bewildered and frustrated. I cannot see my way through the pain, and I'm worried about seeing people who have hurt me this Christmas. I pray You would show me how much You love me, how much You identify with my pain. Give me the courage to flourish in the place I'd rather not be. Give me the strength to forgive and move on. Help me to see You are at work, even when it doesn't seem evident. Restore, renew, and rebuild my broken heart today. Amen.

Activity

Write the name of someone you need to forgive on a paper airplane. Practice flying it away from you as you choose, again, to forgive.

Work to bring peace and prosperity wherever you are—even in dysfunctional family gatherings over the holidays. Choose to bloom where you've been planted, even if the planting is not your choice.

DAY 26

Provision

And my God will meet all your needs according

to the riches of his glory in Christ Jesus.

obin lost her job a month before Christmas. Initially she panicked. How would she put presents under the tree? With the winter being extra cold, how would she pay her heating bill? And what about all those end-of-the-year bills? Every morning as Christmas neared, she started the day in panic, only to see God's faithfulness throughout the day. In this unsteady time of joblessness, she found that panic seldom served her.

She learned several things on her journey of trust that month.

She realized that God is her provider. We err when we think it's all up to us to provide. While hard work and industry are important, ultimately God is our provider. He can provide through our own jobs, through strange circumstances, through others, through supernatural means. Robin experienced this in surprising ways. Unexpected checks. The kindness of strangers. Friends at church who have continued to pray for and support her family. When you face financial stress, it's so lovely to know that God sees, and He will provide for you. It may not be the way you envision His provision, but it comes—sometimes in surprising packages.

Robin also learned she didn't need much. Although her children would have called her frugal before, it's truer today. Robin pared down her budget to the essentials. She didn't purchase extra stuff. Her family seldom went out to eat (and then with a coupon). She diligently changed service providers to lessen her bills and negotiated with the gas company to stretch out her payments. Instead of throwing money at things, she added more logic and time and prayer. She learned important lessons about how much she really needed, and how many wants had fueled her past lifestyle. She learned to settle down into the season, appreciating things that didn't cost money—a drive to see the lights, sitting next to the tree, reading Christmas stories, baking cookies from scratch.

Losing her job helped Robin internalize this truth: humbleness equaled great gain. It wasn't easy being dependent. To always be the one who financially struggles. To say no so many times. But Robin discovered what true joy is, particularly during the holiday season. It resulted from engaging with others, bearing their burdens, and finding empathy for those who suffer—and there were plenty of people like that in her life, especially around Christmas. Now Robin has so much more compassion for anyone who has lost a job. Her heart practically leaps out of her chest for anyone else facing financial worry. So, she's become grateful for this humble, dependent time, and she has a greater understanding of what it must have been like for Joseph and Mary as they struggled to find a place to give birth. They, too, had few resources.

Robin may not be able to financially give as she'd like, but she can give her time. She can pray, listen, and intercede. She can be grateful to those who have also helped her family, thanking them and Jesus.

The truth? God is your provider. No matter what financial stress you face today, know down deep that He sees you and will pull you through.

Jesus, I want to get to the place where I truly believe You see me, and You will take note of our needs. You are good, and You are my provider, even as Christmas bills loom. Help me be a good steward of everything You've given me. Amen.

Activity

Volunteer at a local soup kitchen. It will help put your current situation into perspective.

We err when we think it's all up to us to provide. While hard work and industry are important, ultimately God is our provider.

DAY 27

Be Kind This
Christmas

Or do you show contempt for the riches of his kindness,

forbearance and patience, not realizing that God's

kindness is intended to lead you to repentance?

Kindness thrives in a haven-like environment. As we approach the holidays, we'll inevitably welcome more people into our homes. The question is, will those homes be havens or places of discord? How can we foster kindness so well that we treat our loved ones even *better* than we treat strangers?

God's kindness woos us toward repentance. Not His wrath, judgment, or power. His kindness. Which then begs the question: Why is it that we're kinder to strangers than we are to our own families? Why do we think that shouting, belittling, and shaming our family members or friends will bring about true repentance?

We need to take a breather and rethink the way we approach the people we love. Our kindness will bring about heart change. How we love matters.

Sharon experienced this. One of her children, Shane, had a hard time as finals approached before Christmas break. This was not an issue of brainpower, but rather an issue of effort. Sharon could have berated Shane and told him to try harder. (And she wanted to.) But instead, she sensed God telling her to slow down, ask questions, listen, and have a quiet conversation. The end result was that Shane felt heard. Together, they uncovered the "why" of his fear, and ended up praying for each other. Kindness leads to open conversations. It leads to understanding. It opens doors for relationship.

As Sharon discovered, listening can be the doorway to someone's heart. Instead of immediately assuming the worst, we can take a pause, ask a question, then sit back and listen. Listening is dignifying. It welcomes relationship.

We have a unique opportunity this Christmas to *really* listen. Once we've spent time with someone and heard her heart, we have gained valuable information. Perhaps we found that our loved one really needs a new coat, so we give it as a gift. Or an elderly relative is lonely, so we write cards or sing Christmas carols at his residence. Listening, then acting, will not only display kindness to the people in our lives, but it will increase our joy during the season.

God's kindness does amazing things in our own lives. Why not return the favor to those we love?

Jesus, first I need to really internalize Your kindness. Teach me what it means that You've been kind to me. Let that guide the way I treat the people in my life. Help me to listen well and act on the needs of those I love. Amen.

Activity

Today, when you encounter a stranger, be excessively kind. This may be in line at the grocery store, on the phone with customer service, or as you go about your day. Share your experience with a loved one later in the day.

> Listening can be the doorway to someone's heart. Instead of immediately assuming the worst, we can pause, ask a question, then sit back and listen. Listening is dignifying. It welcomes relationship.

DAY 28

A Conspiracy of
Encouragement

When he saw the crowds, he had compassion on them,

because they were harassed and helpless,

like sheep without a shepherd.

MATTHEW 9:36

Have you ever experienced Christmas stress? Lines snake around the store and don't seem to move, people cut you off in holiday traffic, and you worry about how to pay for everything. Have you felt harassed and helpless, a victim of a string of fretful days as you prepare for company? In each moment, remember this: if you're overwhelmed, the best way to overcome your stress is to find someone else who is stressed and serve him or her. In other words, provide the very thing you need to someone else in need.

Brenda felt as if her world were imploding. Bills too high. Patience too low. Frustration growing by the minute, as Christmas loomed. What Brenda needed was encouragement to continue on with her preparations. She needed to know God saw her. She needed to be reminded that God is the provider—not her. But the needed words of encouragement didn't come.

Brenda reminded herself that it was more blessed to give than to receive, so she started her own conspiracy of encouragement that Christmas. She took to Twitter on a kindness rampage, her heart welling up for people she knew. Faithful people. People so beloved of God. She felt a little like Jesus must have felt in today's verse, her heart filled with compassion for people without a shepherd—aimless and hurting. She tried her best to publicly point out beautiful things about others, taking time to pray for and revel in these amazing Twitter friends. It became such a joyful experience that Brenda nearly felt addicted to the practice.

Then she ventured on to Facebook and wrote encouragement on a few friends' timelines, publicly praising those who have been so very faithful to Jesus during hard times. They were Brenda's heroes, and she wanted them to know.

Next she called a widow who would be without her spouse that Christmas for the first time in their twenty-three year marriage and offered to pray for her during their conversation. Once she said amen, a little more of her frustration flew away.

Brenda's underlying sadness finally abated. It didn't go away completely. Sometimes life is so full of hard circumstances, you can't crawl completely out. But the sting of the season's craziness, and the pervasive feeling that she would always be sad in the midst of it, evaporated. She gave what she needed to receive, and in so doing, received far more.

Are you hurting today? Wishing someone would encourage you as you face another stressful Christmas season? There are no guarantees that someone will take the time to help you. But here are two important truths: God will lift your head, and you have the choice to become the hero you need. Start encouraging someone right now. It doesn't take much time. But it could change a life. Maybe even yours.

Jesus, open my eyes to see those who are hurting around me. I'm already well aware of my own panic, and sometimes that blinds me to the pain of others. Help me see them as You do, as sheep needing a shepherd. Show me who to encourage today. Amen.

Activity

If you're on social media, choose one venue (Facebook, Instagram, Twitter, etc.) to create your own encouragement rampage. Publicly praise people you admire. Bring encouragement to someone's page. If you're not on social media, compose an e-mail or handwrite a card to someone, specifically encouraging him or her.

> You have the choice to become the hero you need: start encouraging someone right now. It doesn't take much time. But it could change a life. Maybe even yours.

DAY 29

The Gift of Time

Be very careful, then, how you live—not as unwise but

as wise, making the most of every opportunity,

because the days are evil. Therefore do not be foolish,

but understand what the Lord's will is.

EPHESIANS 5:15–17

Ellie faced a crisis of faith. After raising her children and finding herself with an empty nest, she no longer felt useful. Without her family to pour herself into, what could she do? Her husband had recently retired, so their income was limited; she had few resources to offer anyone. Christmas only augmented her feelings of worthlessness. To make matters worse, many of her friends and extended family members had moved away, leaving her lonely, and a favorite uncle had died the year before, opening afresh the wound already in her heart. How could she make a difference in the world while she watched her circle of friendships and family growing ever smaller?

Her friend Leslie recommended that she call their local Meals on Wheels chapter because the nonprofit was terribly understaffed, and during the holidays, their deliveries typically increased. Initially Ellie let discouragement prevent her from volunteering. Surely they wouldn't want someone like her delivering food, someone well past her prime. What could she give? She didn't even like driving. But as Thanksgiving passed and the need grew, Ellie picked up the phone and called. Her voice shook as she offered her assistance.

Four days later, after a little training, Ellie started driving to people's homes. Initially she thought of herself as merely a delivery woman, simply knocking on the door (like a UPS worker), delivering the meal, then leaving. But that all changed at her first home—an elderly man, Bill, opened the door and beckoned her inside. She sat while Bill offered her coffee. He shared about his own loneliness, how he felt it more keenly around the holidays. Ellie nodded. She understood.

House after house, the routine was the same—each person asking her to stay, to listen, to give of her time. The day flew by quickly, and Ellie was beaming when she came home.

From that moment on, Ellie felt useful again. She may not have had money or gifts or even her children nearby. But she did have time, and she made the most of it—giving selflessly to those who desperately needed both a meal and a listening ear.

Don't underestimate the power of the gift of time this Christmas. In a flash, presents are opened, oohed over, then typically forgotten. But people remember kindness. They remember experiences. The gift of time is the kind of gift that stays with folks. So, stay alert, and make the most of your time this year.

Jesus, show me those people in my life who need my time. Help me to serve them with joy, making the most of the time You've graciously given me on this earth. I realize that in serving others this way, my joy increases. Amen.

Activity

The next time someone wants to carry on a conversation with you (the checkout line, as you go about your day), stop and take a moment to listen. Find creative ways to give of your time this year.

> Don't underestimate the power of the gift of time this Christmas. In a flash, presents are opened, oohed over, then typically forgotten. But people remember kindness.

DAY 30

You Are Beautiful Enough

I care very little if I am judged by you or by any human

court; indeed, I do not even judge myself.

1 CORINTHIANS 4:3

Emily and Shelley sat across from Lori at their annual Christmas breakfast—a tradition they started several years ago to celebrate their friendship at their favorite bakery. As they reminisced about the year, Lori said, "I am so disappointed in myself. I didn't achieve any of my goals this year, and I can't seem to get it together."

Shelley reached out and laid her hand on Lori's. "I don't know anyone else who is harder on herself than you are. I'd love to see you offer yourself more grace." Emily nodded.

Lori could see it hurt her friends when she put herself down, but it was a habit, something she found herself doing continually, for any reason—or none at all.

That morning Lori's husband had told her she was beautiful, but she could not receive the compliment because she was so upset that she had gained weight over Thanksgiving. Surely he must be just as disgusted with her as she was with herself, she thought. "I wish you would just believe me," he'd said.

Now, as she sat across from Emily and Shelley, she remembered another thing she could share to prove to them she wasn't as good as they thought she was. Her guilt loomed large. "If you only knew all the things I do wrong," she told them, "you wouldn't offer grace."

Emily laughed. "Oh, sister," she said. "We all feel that way. None of us measures up to our impossibly high standards."

Shelley nodded. "The key is letting go of those negative thoughts and replacing them with truths. You are free. You are forgiven. You are loved."

Lori wanted to believe her friends, wanted to stop yelling at herself. She longed to be free like that. "I need your help," she admitted.

"Of course," Emily said, then took a bite of her muffin before continuing.

"Jesus already took your sin," she went on, mouth still half-full. "You're safe in His arms. Truly. You don't need to humiliate yourself. Jesus has already forgiven you, and He loves you." The three continued their conversation through two more pots of coffee and several more pastries as Shelley and Emily encouraged Lori with reminders of who she was in Christ, and how *He* saw her.

Lori left their breakfast a little lighter on her feet. Her heart lightened. Could it be that Jesus truly loved her? That she didn't need to be so harsh to herself, trying to make herself acceptable when she was already accepted?

The truth is: relentless self-shaming doesn't produce fruit—love, joy, peace, patience, kindness, gentleness, faithfulness, self-control. Instead, this kind of self-put-down breeds hatred, sadness, discord, impatience (with yourself), harshness, fickleness, and out-of-control thoughts.

In contrast, what does the voice of God bring? Conviction, yes, but with peace. Hope. Love. Affection. Tenderness. Deep kindness. *Grace.*

So, if you're spending your internal life yelling at yourself, perhaps that means the voice of God has been crowded out. And maybe it's time to dethrone that voice and, instead, enthrone God's sweet, gentle, encouraging voice.

Here's the truth: you are amazing. You're beautiful. You are made in the image of our amazing God, who offers amazing grace. Perhaps it's time, as you face another turn of the year, to accept His grace.

Jesus, help me to see myself as You do—as a child loved by You. Instead of concentrating on my mistakes, help me to say kind words to myself. I trust You to help me. Amen.

Activity

Write a letter to yourself about your struggle with being kind to yourself. Seal the envelope and put today's date on it; then open it next year on the same day to see how much you've grown.

Here's the truth: you are amazing. You're beautiful. You are made in the image of our amazing God, who offers amazing grace.

The Perfect Perspective

Finally, brothers and sisters, whatever is true, whatever

is noble, whatever is right, whatever is pure, whatever

is lovely, whatever is admirable—if anything is excellent

or praiseworthy—think about such things.

PHILIPPIANS 4:8

Christmastime brought out the scrooge in Elizabeth. Instead of seeing everything with wide-eyed wonder, she complained. The roads were too crowded. People stood in her way. Her obligations increased as Christmas Day drew near. And all the commercialism needled at her. That's how each Advent season progressed—until little Selma came into her life.

Elizabeth's next-door neighbors, Jim and Liz, had adopted Selma from an orphanage overseas, and now the four-year-old would experience her first Christmas with a family. The little girl struggled to walk with a walker, having suffered from malnutrition as an infant. Her new mom and dad were quickly making both her health and her life better.

For reasons Elizabeth didn't understand, Selma had taken to her, and often invited her on her new family's outings, small and large. Jim and Liz also loved Elizabeth, so they were quick to offer invitations of their own.

The first week of December, they all went together to their town's annual Christmas parade, something Elizabeth had dreaded at first. So many people! So much traffic! And the weather—so cold! But as Selma slipped her mittened hand into Elizabeth's while the local high school band marched to the tune of "Jingle Bells," Elizabeth caught herself smiling. When Santa threw candy canes, Elizabeth scurried to grab one, then proudly handed it to a smiling Selma.

On another day, Elizabeth watched as Selma worked her way onto Santa's lap—a huge effort. But her smile was as wide as her resolve. After telling Santa her Christmas wish and scrambling back down from his lap, she motioned for Elizabeth to follow her through the mall, packed with people. Instead of growing frustrated at the crowd, Elizabeth noticed how people stopped for Selma, how they smiled at her. The afternoon, instead of being laborious and stressful, ended up being the highlight of her Christmas.

Because of Selma's sweet spirit, Elizabeth realized that up to now, her perspective had tainted everything. She could choose to settle back into her pessimistic ways, barking her stress to anyone within earshot, or she could see things from Selma's childlike perspective. When she did that, the world morphed from monotonous to magical.

You have that choice today too. As this world seems to career off-kilter and the demands of the season press in hard, you have the opportunity to choose your perspective. While news cycles remind us of everything that's wrong with this world, there is also much that is true, noble, right, pure, lovely, admirable, excellent, and praiseworthy. Fixing our minds on those things will not only lighten the burden we carry this season, but it will deepen our Christmas enjoyment.

Jesus, I need a change in perspective. Forgive me for dwelling on everything that's bad in the world and the season. This Christmas, please help me see what noble and amazing things You are doing. I want to fix my mind on what is good. Amen.

Activity

Find a local community event to attend this year—a Christmas parade, a carriage ride, a tree-lighting ceremony. Instead of rushing through it, stop to consider the goodness all around you. Ask God to re-orient your perspective so you'll be prone to revel in what is good and noble.

While news cycles remind us of everything that's wrong with this world, there is also much that is true, noble, right, pure, lovely, admirable, excellent, and praiseworthy. Fixing our minds on those things will not only lighten the burden we carry this season, but it will deepen our Christmas enjoyment.